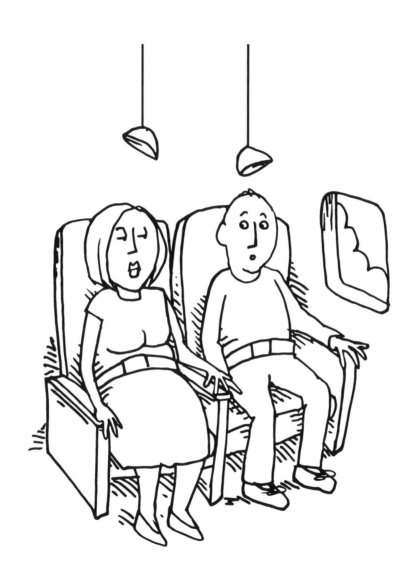

ISBN 979-8-218-02267-9

Library of Congress Control Number: 2023917060

Published by New Twist Press, Los Angeles, California

Book design by Kate Basart/*unionpageworks.com*

A custom edition of this book is the rainmaker you've been looking for.

Reach us at *NewTwist**.Press*

Last  List

Plan B for the Invincible

RICH LIPPMAN

illustrations by
DENNIS GORIS

NEW TWIST.PRESS

To your long life.

WHY SOME OF YOU WILL STOP READING HERE

A confession by the author.

No one ever wants to start a Will.

That included me.

Until I figured out why.

It's not so much what's messing with your thinking.

It's what's missing.

Creativity.

Creativity to inspire those you care about.

Creativity to inspire yourself, too.

In ways most experts never think to tell you.

But this book will.

Read on.

IT'S NOW ABOUT LOVE.

BUT LET'S FIRST SHOO THOSE 4 ELEPHANTS IN THE ROOM

1. THE 'D' WORD

2. THE TAB

3. THE CHOICE

4. THE DISCLAIMER

THE 'D' WORD

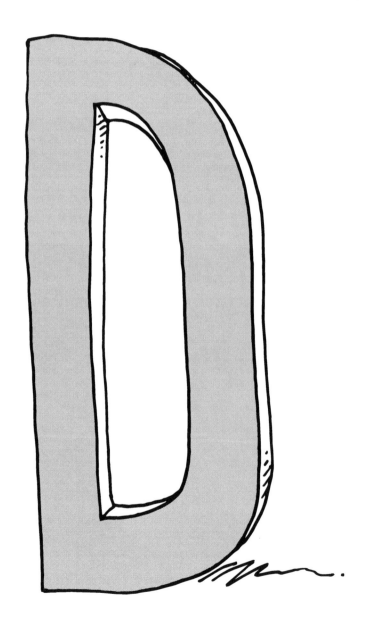

Ever hear your name in the same breath as "D-d-death?"

Spooky, huh?

And who's dropping the D-word like there's no tomorrow?

Your lawyer, since that's what you're talking about.

For many, the D-word stings like tiny darts to the ear.

Luckily, we've got your warm protective earmuffs right here:

JUST SAY IT.

Again.

And again.

Out loud this time.

Feel better?

That's the death of your fear.

THE TAB

How you gonna pay, pal?

You: (nervously) "How much??"

Lawyer: (coolly) "It depends."

You: (more nervously) *"On what??"*

On this: Is your life one big reality show? Are your state laws straight out of the Dark Ages? Is anything NOT overpriced in your town? Do your top-level challenges call for top-shelf experts? Are you famous for needing *waaay* too much hand-holding?

Then start here . . .

- TALK WITH A FEW LICENSED HAND-HOLDERS IN YOUR STATE.
- CHOOSE THE ONES SPECIALIZING IN ESTATE PLANNING.
- LOOK FOR FOUR-STAR REVIEWS.
- ASK THEM WHAT'S INCLUDED—AND WHAT ISN'T.
- SEE IF THEIR FIRST MEETING IS FREE.
- THEN CHOOSE THE MOST QUALIFIED EXPERT YOU CAN AFFORD.

And if you two happen to click?

PRICELESS.

THE CHOICE

Real Lawyer vs. Online Will?

WILLS
'R US

Most lawyers don't like online Wills.

A few do.

They're the ones cleaning up on cleaning up online Wills that went bust at the bitter end.

SO WHICH IS BEST FOR YOU . . . PROFESSIONALS OR PIXELS?

Is your life easy breezy?

Money kinda tight?

Then you'll save big bucks going with a quality online Will.

Is your life rarely easy and tornado-force breezy?

Sibling rivals? Thorny finances? Special-needs kids? Slippery kin (with sticky fingers)?

Then the CHOICE is easy breezy . . .

Professionals.

Estate-planning professionals.

LEGAL SPEAK

The author and publisher do not assume, and hereby disclaim, any liability to the reader, or any other party, for any loss, damage, or disruption caused by any errors or omissions, whether such errors or omissions result from negligence, inaccuracy, incompleteness, or any other cause. This book is a source of information only, and not a substitute for personalized legal and financial counsel from licensed estate-planning and financial-planning professionals, whom the reader is strongly advised to seek out. The reader accepts full responsibility for their own choices, plans, actions, and outcomes.

PLAIN ENGLISH

YOU ARE RESPONSIBLE FOR YOU. Find quality, qualified legal and financial navigators licensed in your state, or you'll be up that famous creek without a paddle. Or a canoe.

Q: WHAT'S IN A LAST BUCKET?

A: THE CONTENTS

THE OVERSPILL

Create *Aha!*

Last Bucket List .com

HELLO!

(From the last lawyer in here.)

Clayton Cruse

Estate Planning Attorney
The Estate, PLLC

I LOVE WHAT I DO.

That's because helping people safeguard their families is what Estate Planning is all about.

Trouble is, Step One can feel a bit overwhelming for people just starting out.

Lawyers know.

WE'VE SEEN THOSE EYES GLAZE OVER.

What we all needed was a friendly welcome to the mission of Estate Planning—like this book.

I hope you'll feel better prepared.

I hope you'll feel inspired.

I hope we'll see you at Step Two.

"I intend to
live forever.
So far . . .
so good."

—STEVEN WRIGHT

CHAPTER 1

YOUR SUPERHEROES

Worth a fortune someday.

Psst: If your Superheroes ever dress up like this, get yourself some new Superheroes.

WHO WOULDN'T WANT THEIR OWN LEGION OF SUPERHEROES PROTECTING THEM?

Not from speeding bullets or intergalactic evildoers—but from some of the toughest jams anyone can face on earth. Yet to earn this powerful protection, you must first rise to a simple challenge . . .

BESTOW SUPERPOWERS ON THE TRUSTED FEW.

Only then can your Superheroes spring into action so they're ready the moment you need them—for as long as you shall live.

SUPERHEROES

Is that **real** legal speak?

Is someone buzzing on kryptonite?? Why not start using the real legal terms—so your lawyer doesn't think you are.

* POWER OF ATTORNEY FOR HEALTHCARE
* POWER OF ATTORNEY FOR FINANCES
* EXECUTOR
* SUCCESSOR TRUSTEE

All play key roles that come to life *only* when you need them. But for now, think up who'd you'd cast in each role—so you can begin buttering them up.

AND YOUR SUPERHERO NOMINEES ARE . . .

 POWER OF ATTORNEY FOR HEALTHCARE to carry out your wishes if ever you're facing a real health emergency—just as *you'd* want them carried out.

 POWER OF ATTORNEY FOR FINANCES to look after your money business if ever you're down for the count—just as *you'd* want it looked after.

 EXECUTOR to sort out your Will once you're gone, and take on the pleasure of Probate. *Wait . . .* Probate??

 SUCCESSOR TRUSTEE to step in after you're gone— or too far gone—to carry out your Living Trust. *Wait . . .* what??

WHO'LL FILL YOUR SUPERHERO BOOTS?

Sometimes the right people are obvious. Other times the obvious people are anything but right. It all comes down to values, timing, availability, trust.

And who melts from your buttering up.

PROTIPS

Superheroes

⭐ Choose 4 people you trust—or one person for all 4 roles.

⭐ Choose a couple of trusted backups for each role as well.

⭐ Any kids? Teens? Add a Guardian Superhero to your Legion, too (page 136).

★ Superheroes aren't allowed to give their superpowers away.

★ Superheroes aren't allowed to change your wishes.

★ But **YOU** can always change your Superheroes.

★ If you don't trust 'em — don't choose 'em!

POP QUIZ

What the heck does "Estate Planning" mean anyway?

CIRCLE ONE:

a. It's sorta about real estate.

b. It's kinda about mansions.

c. It's only for millionaires.

d. None of the above.

If you circled **d**, you scored better than the genius who came up with the gibberish title "estate planning." The first reason so many run from it is they don't know what it means. The next hundred reasons? Who cares?

YOU'RE HOLDING THE ANSWER KEY.

MARLON BRANDO

THE CASE OF THE EMPTY PROMISE.

The legendary actor confided to his longtime housekeeper that after he died, she'd come into

A SMALL FORTUNE.

But somehow, his words never made it into his Will. So after the actor passed, his housekeeper didn't clean up.

SHE JUST KEPT CLEANING.

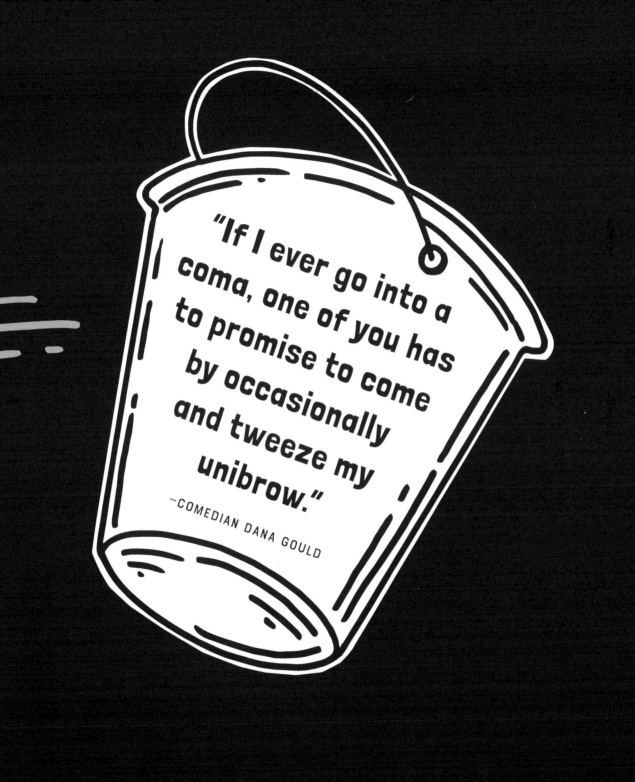

"If I ever go into a coma, one of you has to promise to come by occasionally and tweeze my unibrow."

–COMEDIAN DANA GOULD

CHAPTER 2

TREAT ME RIGHT

In case
What If . . .

Becomes
. . . What Now?

EVERYONE LOVES LADY LUCK.

Everyone loathes her sister.

That's Miss Fortune, the stealthy hellcat who delights in throwing the nicest people under the bus.

LITERALLY.

Cross paths with either sister, and your life changes in a flash.

So hold on to that daydream of peeling out in a cherry-red Ferrari 812 GTS.

But also test-drive the armored vehicle revving for you on the next page.

THE HEALTHCARE DIRECTIVE: YOUR VOICE WHEN IT'S NEEDED.

If Miss Fortune ever leaves you speechless, this short, free, do-it-yourself-in-advance legal vehicle is how you'll still be able to speak for yourself.

That's because it holds your own medical decisions, so doctors will know what you want if—*and only if*—you're caught up in an unforeseen medical jam.

No Healthcare Directive?

Then someone in your family will have to take over your medical decisions for you.

But who?

Squeamish spouse? Slacker kid? Salivating heir??

How about the one who knows you better than all of them put together?

(PSST . . . YOU!)

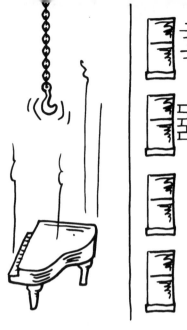

WHAT DOES A HEALTHCARE DIRECTIVE ASK YOU?

WHO do you trust to direct your medical decisions?

WHAT are those decisions?

WHO'LL BE YOUR SUPERHERO "WHO"?

Who do you trust to understand your wishes, honor them, and keep their cool in a tsunami of doctors, nurses, bean-counters and your pushiest relatives?

Narrow it down: Good communicator. Easily reachable. Polite yet assertive. Hears clearly. Listens well. Over 18. Doesn't work for your healthcare provider.

ISN'T A COSMO KRAMER.

Many folks naturally choose their life partner, but anyone you know and trust works well, too.

Then write in a couple of reliable backups, just in case.

And if your situation ever changes, just change your Healthcare Directive.

It doesn't ask or care why.

WHAT'LL BE YOUR "WHAT"?

Deep breath.

How would you want doctors to care for you if ever you were unable to communicate?

How would you wish to be treated . . . have your comfort tended . . . your dignity upheld?

When would you say it's time to surrender the good fight, and pull the plug?

Or not.

Tough questions, for sure.

Only one thing makes this less difficult.

Doctors having your signed Healthcare Directive in hand, so they know your wishes, which they must follow.

BECAUSE IT'S THE LAW.

Think how much this one piece of paper could mean for you—especially if you and your family rarely agree on anything.

JUST BETWEEN US . . .

Here, we simply call this form a Healthcare Directive. But your state likely calls it a tongue twister all its own:

- **POA OR MPOA (MEDICAL POWER OF ATTORNEY)**
- **ADVANCE DIRECTIVE**
- **PERSONAL DIRECTIVE**
- **ADVANCE HEALTH CARE DIRECTIVE**
- **FIVE WISHES (BEST OF ALL)**

What's more, your state may split the form into two tongue twisters instead of one:

- **LIVING WILL & DESIGNATION OF A HEALTH CARE SURROGATE**
- **DECLARATION & DURABLE POWER OF ATTORNEY FOR HEALTH CARE**
- **DOCUMENT DIRECTING HEALTH CARE & HEALTH CARE PROXY**

Luckily, these forms are easy to find. Ask your attorney, financial planner or healthcare provider, or search online—once you've figured out which tongue twister your state calls it.

TONGUE-TIED?

Some conversations are tough.

Like this one.

The talk where you clue in trusted family about what you've written into your Healthcare Directive—even if you're certain they'll think they'll know.

(They won't.)

UNTIE YOUR TONGUE.

Let's end those anxious middle-of-the-night monologues with your pillow.

Accept this invitation from today's leading conversation consultants, so you won't keep putting off this important talk for, um, ever.

And don't worry about how much these world-class experts charge for their advice. You can afford it.

Just download the Conversation Project's free Conversation Starter Guide. It comes complete with everything you need to break the ice.

EXCEPT THE DRINKS.

PROTIPS

Healthcare Directive

⇨ A "Superhero Who" is called a POA, MPOA, HCPA, Healthcare Power of Attorney, Proxy or Agent everywhere else.

⇨ All photocopies of your signed Healthcare Directive are legit.

⇨ Give copies to your Who, your trusted family member(s), your healthcare provider, attorney, and any official state registry.

⇨ Revisit what you wrote in your form every decade — sooner if your life changes.

⇨ Baffled? Confused? There's a clearer form out there if you look online.

⇨ On your phone's emergency screen, note where someone can find your Directive.

➡ If you do **only one thing** from this book, **do this.**

_____
_____

CHAPTER 3

TOSS YOURSELF A LIFELINE

Your memories can be a real game changer.

STAY WITH THIS FOR A MOMENT . . .

Suppose . . . one day . . . you end up in a coma.

Perish that thought.

But what if a friend could try something that might bring you around? Something not even on many doctors' radar. Something so easy, it's as simple as deputizing your friend to:

- RETELL HEARTWARMING (OR EMBARRASSING) STORIES FROM YOUR LIFE.
- UNCAP A SCENT THAT REMINDS YOU OF A CERTAIN PLACE . . . OR A SPECIAL SOMEONE.
- PLAY YOU THE SONG YOU FELL IN LOVE TO.

IT'S WORTH A TRY, RIGHT?

Especially since it's been shown to work.

CAN MEMORIES REALLY "REBOOT" A BRAIN?

Yes they can.

Medical researchers recently invited families of coma patients to record deeply personal stories from the lives of their loved ones.

Several times each day, these familiar voices telling heartfelt tales were played for the patients through headsets.

No drugs. No surgeries. No cost.

Just memories.

C'MON . . . DID THIS ACTUALLY WORK?

The patients didn't exactly sit up and ask for a sandwich, but to everyone's amazement and relief, many came around more quickly and easily.

That's more than a triumph . . .

It's worthy of a special place in your Healthcare Directive to list a few of the wonderful memories that live in your head.

WHAT LIGHTS UP YOUR CIRCUITS?

WORDS? Favorite poem, psalm, anecdote, family story, bible passage, book excerpt, song lyric, inside joke, soft whispered intimacy, personal triumph—or big-time blooper.

SOUNDS? Rousing Broadway showstopper, wedding song, power rocker, childhood ice-cream jingle, ASMR tingle, Game 7 victory—or brainteasing earworm.

SCENTS? (With doctor's okay.) Mom's famous pie, Dad's infamous cologne, fresh-baked bread, sick-day menthol rub, beach-day sunscreen—or peatiest whisky.

ADD YOURS TO YOUR HEALTHCARE DIRECTIVE.

Flip toward the back and find the "Other Wishes" section. Then make yours known.

Too little space?

Write, "See attached," and take all the space you need.

And whether your deepest memories are ever replayed for recovery, comfort, hope or strength, may yours bring you a sense of peace when you might need it most.

CHAPTER 4

THE LOVING GIFT WITHIN

Be the grand prize of life.

Ever slam into this question at the DMV?

> ❏ **Do you want to register your decision to be an organ, eye, and tissue donor?**

WHAT?!! Now? *In the middle of this three-ring circus*??

Good questions.

DMV wondered, too.

So they hired a pricey consultant to survey cranky citizens during DMV meltdowns to see if they minded being asked to register to donate their organs.

And what did they discover?

They wasted their money.

HEY DMV— ASK US LIKE THIS:

If an unwell patient ever needs an organ to stay alive, will you donate yours once you're no longer using it?

☐ Yes ☐ No

If **YOU** ever need an organ to stay alive, will you accept someone else's once they're no longer using it?

☐ Yes ☐ No

If both answers don't agree, go to the back of the line.

DONATING ORGANS: GIVING THAT MEANS LIVING.

Until science figures out how to grow working organs in a lab, second chances at life for many often come down to a simple *yes* . . .

From the just-deceased.

So instead, they ask the living. On a day they might be feeling on top of the world.

Or standing in an endless line at the DMV.

But is there really *ever* a good time to ask? Let's find out:

WILL YOU GIFT YOUR ORGANS?

Perhaps you already have.

Then accept a hearty *thank you* from the over 100,000 folks holding on for dear life, on any given day, in every given year.

Haven't? Then ask yourself how those same 100,000 would sound cheering and clapping wildly for you.

Find out.

Say *yes.*

DONATING TISSUE: MORE GIFTING WORTH GIVING.

In life, there are two types of tissue . . .

The kind we can't wait to throw away. And the kind too many of us throw away.

This is about the second kind. The biological kind.

The kind you can turn into kindness.

BE KIND. SAY YES.

Your courage gifting tissue will someday help doctors:

- HEAL THE BURNED AND INJURED.
- TREAT THE SICK AND WOUNDED.
- ALLOW MORE NATURAL MASTECTOMY RESTORATION.
- REPAIR PHYSICAL ILLS FROM HEAD TO TOE.

POP QUIZ . . .

How many people can you help with just ONE gift of tissue?

☐ 1   ☐ 2   ☐ 3   ☐ 75

(*Hint*: More than three.)

EEEYYYAAA . . . IT'S THE WILLIES!!

You feel 'em. We ALL feel 'em.

They're natural, expected, creepy, uncomfortable.

And you can more easily shoo them away if your state lets you gift only to:

- LIFESAVING, RECONSTRUCTION, EDUCATION AND RESEARCH.
- NONPROFIT ORGANIZATIONS.
- HEALTHCARE IN THE U.S.A.

Shoo 'em even more if your state lets you hold back:

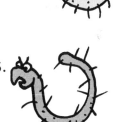

- ANYTHING YOU WISH TO KEEP WITH YOU.
- ANYTHING THAT MIGHT GO TO PLUMP-UP LIPS—OR ANYTHING NOT PLUMPY ENOUGH BETWEEN THE HIPS.

ONE MORE WILLIE WIPER

For lots of medical reasons, 99.7% of all organ gifters will never get to be actual donors.

So thank you anyway for your generous *yes*.

Try not to feel TOO rejected.

PROTIPS

Gifting

 You're never too old, too fragile or too sexy to gift.

 Nearly every faith blesses gifting as an act of love and compassion.

 No family ever pays—or gets paid—for gifting.

Q: Why aren't ER doctors told which patients are registered donors?
A: Their only focus is on saving lives.
Q: Can bigwigs and billionaires ever cut to the front of the line?
A: Yes—but only to donate!
VISIT donatelife.net and see how easy it is to register.

JAMES GANDOLFINI

THE CASE OF THE LEGAL-TENDER GRIP.

After the star of *The Sopranos* died, his Will was so riddled with holes, a shadowy character known as Uncle "The Sponge" Sam muscled his way in for

A PIECE OF THE ACTION.

Without a word, this so-called uncle reached through those gaping holes and squeezed the actor's nest eggs so hard—they ended up singing all the way to the bank.

HIGHER THAN ANY SOPRANO.

CHAPTER 5

WHICH SUITS YOU?

- [ ] Last Will?
- [ ] Living Trust?
- [ ] Stark Naked?

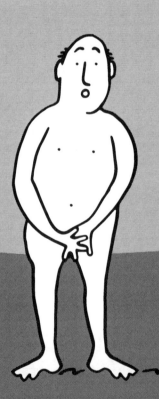

NAKED?

Yup. That's what some businesspeople call clients who risk everything—by doing nothing.

Like going without a Will or Trust.

Naked.

And not in any beachy, frolic-y, skinny-dippy sorta way.

Yet if gallivanting around a tropical paradise sounds good to you, then go ahead and make plans to go.

Right after you finish your Will or Trust.

You'll even have something comfortable and fashionable to wear.

Our tailor will measure you now.

WHICH SUITS YOU: LAST WILL OR LIVING TRUST?

WILLS ARE IDEAL FOR THE SIMPLER LIFE.

If you rent rather than own; if Beverly Hills is for window shopping only; if you're not yet called "sir" or "ma'am" by every clueless teenager; if you want most of your stuff going to your spouse; if you're kid-free; if you don't want to shell out big bucks—then a Last Will & Testament may be for you.

TRUSTS ARE PRETTY MUCH FOR EVERYONE ELSE.

WILLS **MAY SEEM SIMPLER ON THE FRONT END,** but beware the back end. Your family might have to slog to court someday to work it all out, in a potentially costly, drawn-out legal procedure known as Probate. (Probe included.)

TRUSTS **LAUGH AT PROBATE.**

WILLS **COST LESS THAN TRUSTS.**

TRUSTS **COST MORE THAN WILLS—**but laugh at the price of Probate.

WILLS **EVENTUALLY GO PUBLIC FOR THE WORLD TO SEE**—so anyone who feels shafted can take their grudge to a judge.

TRUSTS **STAY SEALED FROM THE WORLD OUTSIDE**—but not from your world inside. In some states, everyone in the Trust gets a full copy, so any spoilsport can also take their grudgin' for a judgin'.

WILLS **INSTANTLY SLIP INTO SLEEP MODE**, but you can usually wake them for changes—such as if you marry, divorce, remarry, have a kid, or disappear into witness protection.

TRUSTS **STAY POWERED UP** to provide advantages over your lifetime (a *Living* Trust). And if yours is "Revocable," you're always free to change it—as well as hold it over the heads of heirs behaving badly.

WILLS **CAN SEND YOUR MONEY ON A ROLLER COASTER RIDE** to places you'd never want it to go—such as into the hands of your formerly happily married kid's future ex—all the way to the farthest branch on that future ex's next spouse's family tree.

TRUSTS **CAN KEEP YOUR MONEY AND VALUABLES TOGETHER WITH YOUR OWN KIDS,** no matter how many marriages they blow through.

WILLS **ARE WHERE YOU SAY WHO YOU WANT RAISING YOUR KIDS** till they turn 18, if ever you can't.

TRUSTS **ARE NOT.** If you have minor kids, you don't need to decide between a Will and a Trust. You likely need both.

WILLS **ARE FOR SETTING UP FINANCIAL SUPPORT FOR YOUR MINOR KIDS TILL THEY TURN 18.** Then they're free to stuff all your leftover loot into a shiny new convertible and zoom straight to Vegas, baby!

TRUSTS **ARE ALSO FOR SETTING UP FINANCIAL SUPPORT FOR YOUR MINOR KIDS.** And when they turn 18, they're also free to zoom straight to Vegas—minus any of your leftover loot if you've said it stays in the Trust till . . . *oh* . . . there's a diploma on the wall, baby!

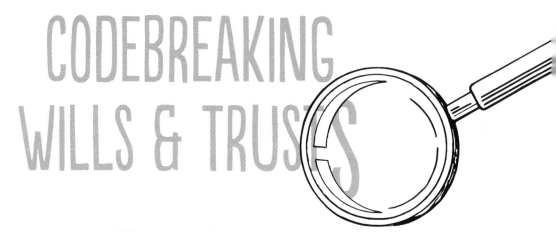

CODEBREAKING WILLS & TRUSTS

Last Will and Testament

TESTATOR—YOU, the Will's creator.

EXECUTIONER—NO ONE. A rookie misreading of Executor.

EXECUTOR—NOT YOU. Whoever you name to carry out your Will.

BENEFICIARY—NOT YOU. Whoever you name to inherit your stuff.

INTESTATE—NOT YOU. Unless you never finish this book and leave no Will or Trust.

PROBATE—The courthouse grind for settling Wills—and unsettling families.

YOU WERE LISTED AS THE **EXECUTOR**.

Living Trust

TRUSTOR—**YOU,** the creator of the Trust. (a.k.a. Trustmaker, Settlor, Grantor, Moneybags).

TRUSTEE—**YOU** again, or someone you name to manage your Trust.

BENEFICIARY—**YOU** again! At least as long as you're kickin'. Then, it's who you say gets your stuff.

SUCCESSOR TRUSTEE—**NOT YOU.** The person you name to manage your Trust once you or the Trustee no longer can.

REVOCABLE—A word with two pronunciations that means the Trust can be changed—by forking out for more billable hours.

IRREVOCABLE—Another two-pronunciation word that means you likely can't change the Trust without braving flaming hoops and even more billable hours.

CHOOSE YOUR GO-TO

Size–up your Superhero for your Executor or Successor Trustee.

Who'll be best at handling your bills, debts, taxes, investments and barking beneficiaries once you can't? Run your candidates through this quick quiz and find out.

1. **WHO'S MOST LIKELY TO**

   - Return a lost wallet . . . full?

   - Stand tough . . . when it all hits the fan?

   - Admit when they're lost . . . and ask for directions?

2. **WHO WON'T BE OVERWHELMED BY**

   - Numbers . . . lots of them?

   - Rules . . . too many of them?

   - Emotions . . . a cloudburst of them?

3. **WHICH WAY ARE YOU LEANING?**

   - Oldest child? Or worthiest child?

   - Family member? Or worthiest friend?

   - Iffy insider? Or licensed outsider?

Wait! You're not done yet. Be sure to name a second and third choice, in case your first choice flakes out.

PROTIPS

Living Trust

- 🪙 Think of a new Trust as a large, empty treasure chest.

- 🪙 Now fill it with your money, home, stocks, bonds & valuables.

- 🪙 Leave it unfilled? Then you're simply sitting on a large, overpriced, treasure-less chest.

- Everything you fill into your treasure chest stays 100% yours.

- But leave out your 401(k), IRA & life insurance. Why? Ask only if you've got an hour to kill.

- Name your Trust whatever you want! The zanier you make it, the more you'll freak out the suits at the bank.

- *Revisit your Trust every 5 years—* sooner if your life changes, or they mess with the tax laws again.

PROTIPS

Last Will

⇨ Dramatic Will readings in a stuffy lawyer's office? Only in the movies.

⇨ Unexplained staple holes in a legal Will? Grounds to invalidate.

⇨ "Holographic" Wills don't float in mid-air. It simply means they're handwritten.

➡️ Online Wills are like hospital gowns. Don't assume they'll always cover your butt.

➡️ Dreaming of disinheriting your bitter half? Only if they'll sign your heartless post-nup.

➡️ Leave your IRA, 401(k) & life insurance out of your Will. Don't believe us? Google it.

➡️ **Revisit your Will every 5 years—** sooner if your life changes, or they mess with the tax laws again.

A MYSTERY HEIR

(and his bus-bench lawyer)

THANK YOU FOR →

→ USING A CHEAPO ONLINE WILL.

→ LETTING NO LAWYER REVIEW IT.

→ HAVING NO WITNESSES SIGN IT.

→ SCRIBBLING BOOTLEG CHANGES ALL OVER IT.

→ LEAVING YOUR DNA TEST RESULTS DISCOVERABLE.

→ NOT ANTICIPATING SCOUNDRELS LIKE US.

→ NEVER FINISHING THIS BOOK.

"I just created
a living trust and
I have no idea
what to feed it."

—UNKNOWN

CHAPTER 6

THE TO-DIE-FOR DESSERT

Sweet for your loved ones.

Bittersweet for you.

INHERITANCE PIE
Pre-baked, pre-sliced & pre-served.

INGREDIENTS

All you ever earned, won, inherited, found, mooched, pinched & somehow held onto.

INSTRUCTIONS

1. TOSS INGREDIENTS INTO A LARGE PIE TIN.

2. TOP WITH ALL YOUR DOUGH.

3. PRE-SECTION EVERY PORTION.

4. SET TO BAKE FOR DECADES.

5. SHOO AWAY SALIVATING HEIRS.

6. PIE IS DONE WHEN YOU ARE.

WHY INHERITANCE PIE IS BITTERSWEET TO YOU.

BAM! That's your *life* in that pan.

The risks you took . . . challenges you faced . . . sacrifices you made . . . fools you suffered . . . fortunes you earned . . . losses you swallowed.

Now you're about to carve up the fruits of your labors—and prepare it for those who'll never fully appreciate what you put up with.

And for how long.

SO . . . PAT YOURSELF ON THE BACK.

Toast your wild ride.

Trumpet your triumphs.

Sing from the rooftops.

Dance in the . . .

Hey—Snap out of it!

Go grab the pie cutter.

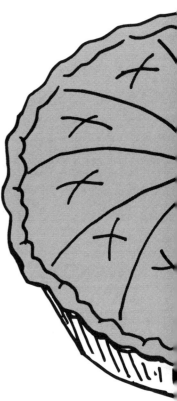

WHY THE *Second* CUT IS THE DEEPEST.

The first cut is a measure of courage.

The second cut is a measure of commitment.

Who'll get the lion's share? Who'll roar without it?
Who's always broke? Who's well off? Who needs schooling?
Who's tough to please? Who'll bellyache at even-steven?

Feel that? It's emotional heartburn—and you haven't even started dividing the family sentimentals yet.

HERE'S YOUR ANTACID . . .

Put down the pie cutter.

Pick up a pen.

Jot down musts.

Add in wants.

Factor in needs.

Factor out perfection.

Stir in love.

Figure in virtue.

Clue in your lawyer.

Then sleep on it.

G'night, friend. Bittersweet dreams.

SHARPEN YOUR PIE CUTTER

13 tips to portion like a pro—
not a sugar freak.

Mmmmm — PIE!

But for this tempting pastry, only the crust should be flaky.

1. Portion with your partner, or solo if you're single.
    NO OTHER SLICERS NEED APPLY.

2. Start by dividing everything into two groups:
    INTANGIBLES & TANGIBLES.

3. INTANGIBLES like money, stock, and whatever lives
    in your financial apps—are best portioned as fixed
    percentages—not fickle dollars.

4. TANGIBLES like houses, cars and all tough-to-split
    valuables—are best portioned by seeing where this
    asterisk leads:*

To your lawyer and financial planner.

5. **EQUAL SLICES FOR ALL KIDS?** What about special needs? Step? Broke? Wealthy? Unhealthy? High-rollin'? High? Estranged? Strange?*

6. **JACKPOT YOUR KIDS IN ONE BIG PAYOUT?** Or dribble it out over time? Can't decide? Then try a tax-free reality show: Surprise each kid with a gift of real money. Then pop the popcorn, sit back, and watch what they do with it. Would the judges care to reconsider any of their generosity?

7. Ever wonder where the rich and famous find their **JUICY LOOPHOLES?***

8. Losing sleep over the seemingly unsolvable? You're not the first. Which means there might be some **READY-MADE LEGAL JUDO** to help you sleep better.*

9. Did you know you can set aside portions for OFFSPRING YET UNSPRUNG?*

10. You can also set aside portions for CAUSES YOU BELIEVE IN—charities, nonprofits, and the good-ol' alma mater.*

11. Heading toward a SIBLING DEMOLITION DERBY 'round the first bend? You're gonna need a bigger guardrail.*

12. PLANTING LANDMINES in your Will? At least tell your family why (page 148).

13. No matter what you say or do, every slice of Inheritance Pie carries its own FOREVER MESSAGE. Make sure it's the one you intend.

Don't try this at home. Ask the experts.

GRABFEST!

What fools these siblings be.

GRANDMA'S BELOVED COOKIE JAR . . .

Empty now but for crumbs of happy childhood memories.

And rapidly filling with venom over who gets to keep it.

Coin flip not cutting it?

Sledgehammer starting to look good?

WHY NOT SETTLE IT LIKE THIS?

Grandma's cookie jar goes to **CHILD A** if you go out on an even day.

Grandma's cookie jar goes to **CHILD B** if the day's an odd one.

It ain't perfect, but it's sporting.

Especially if you dry the tears of the non winner with cash.

And Grandma's consolation cookies.

HOW TO GO FROM

HERO
TO

ZERO

TRUST LEGAL ADVICE FROM A BARSTOOL BLOWHARD.

TAKE FINANCIAL ADVICE FROM A MADOFF KNOCKOFF.

DISH OUT JUICY LOOPHOLES TO SLIPPERY HEIRS.

EXPECT PENTHOUSE WILLS FROM BASEMENT LAWYERS.

LEAVE BUCKETS OF MONEY TO A DIE-HARD SQUANDERER.

FORGET A CARING PROMISE MADE TO A DEAR FRIEND.

LEAVE YOUR EX AS YOUR LIFE INSURANCE BENEFICIARY.

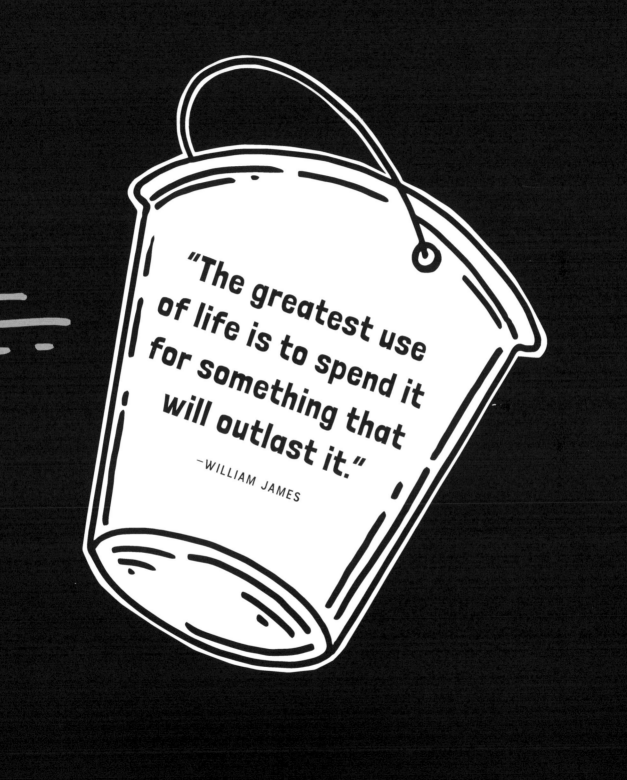

"The greatest use of life is to spend it for something that will outlast it."

—WILLIAM JAMES

CHAPTER 7

MISSIONS OF MEANING

Turn an ordinary bequest into an **extra**ordinary quest.

The dust has settled.
Tears are gone.
Memories linger.
Life goes on.
A letter arrives.
One mission inside . . .

Live life with purpose, passion and pride.

EVER GET TANGLED UP IN "STRINGS ATTACHED?"

Like in that web of fine print on a bank loan, where they take back everything you'd thought was already yours?

Only here, *you* attach the strings—and *you* pull them—to create positive events you wish to take place in the future.

Like paying for a grandkid's education.

Or bankrolling a dream wedding.

Or keeping the family squanderer from blowing their entire inheritance before Happy Hour.

You may pull as you wish, but you may not yank like the control freak who cut off his son if he ever *grew a mustache*.

You can surely guess what the son did then.

Right before parading his face in front of a judge.

The case? Laughed out of court. The son? Walked away wealthy. The mustache? A big F-U Manchu.

MISSIONS OF MEANING ARE STRINGS, TOO.

But they're not for attaching ordinary strings. They're for creating strings of attachment.

Future adventures you dream up, write up, set up—and then, with great pride—pick up the tab for.

With a portion of funds you were giving them anyway!

MINDFUL MISSIONS—NOT MINDLESS VACATIONS.

These are adventures near or far, big or small, playful or profound that you tailor to those you love—designed to bring out the best in each of them:

- **SUNSHINE FOR THE SAD**
- **QUESTS FOR THE CURIOUS**
- **OCTANE FOR THE UNDERDOG**
- **INSPIRATION FOR THE ARTIST**
- **ADRENALINE FOR THE THRILL JUNKIE**
- **OPPORTUNITY FOR THE HEALER**

Best yet, they don't even have to know it's coming.

CREATING MISSIONS OF MEANING

Start with the goal.
Then work backwards.

Dear Brad,

I know how much you care about dogs at the shelter, and there's something I'd like you to do. Go to the hallway hiding place and find the money I left for you there. Whenever you're ready, take it to the shelter where we got Barkley and tell them you want to pay for EVERY adoption till the money runs out. Spaying & neutering, too. Go celebrate a joyful day with lucky families and their lucky lucky pets!

I love you forever Son,

—Dad

My Dear Jordan,

I have a wish for you to make us both proud. I've set aside some seed money to throw a party so you can raise donations for ovarian cancer research. Invite everyone, including my friends. Choose a fun venue, hire a gourmet caterer, get a slammin' band. Set a minimum donation. See if your boss or someone else will match all the funds you raise. Start a crowdfunding page. Make it a worthy bash for a cause we both believe in. Call our lawyer Sam for details. I'll be there with you in spirit . . . then, now and always.

I love you.

Mom

Hi again, Bean . . .

Dad and I are springing a Christmas-time surprise on you. Right before the holiday, put on a goofy Santa hat, head downtown, and hand out these $50's—one or two at a time—to those who might need a little more Christmas cheer. Bring along your friends, maybe post a fun video online. We wish we could be there. We love you always, Bean.

Mom & Dad

P.S. If you get this after you become a parent, you know what to do!

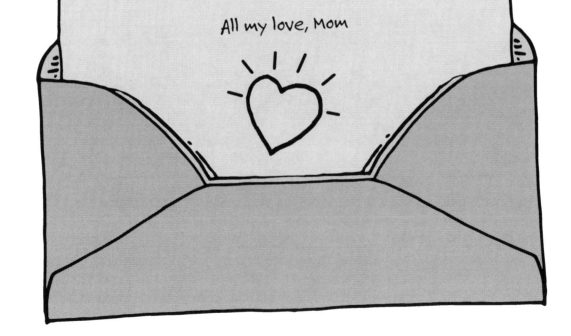

Dear Stevie,

Since you're in charge now, you're also in charge of helping others. Our family has set up a "donor-advised fund" to help those in need, and if you're ready, and willing, and you've turned 18, I'd like you to try your hand at it. Uncle Fred will answer your questions, and our attorney can get you started. I know helping other people live better lives will fill your heart with joy.

All my love, Mom

Dearest PJ,

So you can follow your passion, on top of your inheritance, I've left you some money to open the pottery studio you've always talked about. Our lawyer will help you get started. (Be sure she gets you a good accountant, too!) I'm there with you always. I know you'll make us both proud!

I love you,

Mama

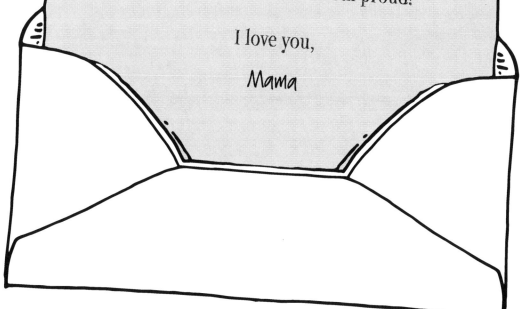

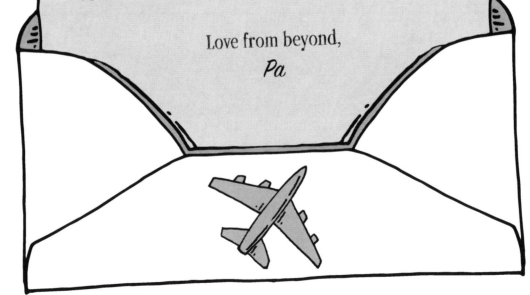

Dear Precious,

I know you're not expecting this, but I've seen to something you've always wanted to do. When the time is right, take a leave of absence and volunteer somewhere in the world, to a place that's calling you, a place that could use your gifts. Roger has the money I set aside to cover your expenses while you're there. Now live!

Take it from me . . . you only do it once.

Love from beyond,
Pa

My Sweet Destiny . . .

Because I always dreamed of going, but never did, I'd like you to visit the land of our heritage for a good while. Live amongst the people, celebrate the culture, savor the food, dance with the locals, and toast us with any long-lost relatives you can locate. And please scatter my ashes on beautiful Lake Chrissie at sunset. Safe travels. My love is with you, always.

Daddy

PROTIPS

Missions of Meaning

✓ Inspire...yes.
Insist...no.

✓ Simple & clear...yes.
Complex & confusing...no.

✓ Lawyer-approved...yes.
Loose ends...no.

✓ Ask a good friend or lawyer to see this through for you.

✓ Be careful not to fan the embers of any smoldering sibling rivalries.

✓ When situations change — change the missions.

✓ **No kids?** Then why not create Missions of Meaning for anyone you love — nieces, nephews, friend's kids, even a mentee.

ODD STRINGS

All true. All odd.
One oddly romantic.

She was buried in a SEXY NIGHTGOWN at the wheel of her hot red Ferrari.

He left millions to **A FEW RANDOS** straight out of the local phone book.

He left his mansion to three lawyers who DESPISED EACH OTHER.

He left millions to a hospital—as long as his **PRESERVED CORPSE** sat in on their board meetings.

He left a bundle to any woman who BIRTHED THE MOST BABIES in the ten years after he passed.

She left **12 MILLION BUCKS** for her dog to chew up.

He willed a fortune to his theatre company—if his skull was used as the PROP IN HAMLET.

She said, "Dress me up like **BOZO THE CLOWN** and put me in an open casket—or no inheritance."

He left several teetotaling clergy equal shares **IN A POPULAR BREWERY.**

He made sure ONE RED ROSE arrived for his wife every morning—for the rest of her life.

CHAPTER 8

UNPACK YOUR PICKLES

What's your 'dill'emma?

Q: What's more important than impressing legal and financial professionals with your questions?

A: Seeing how well they impress you back.

PICK YOUR SPICIEST PICKLES

SPICY PICKLES

FOR THE BLENDED FAMILY

- HOW CAN I KEEP MY MONEY FROM ENRICHING MY EX?

- OR MY SPOUSE'S DISTANT KINFOLK?

- OR MY SPOUSE'S NEXT SPOUSE?

- **WAIT . . . WHO??**

- HOW CAN I BE SURE MY ORIGINAL KIDS WON'T GET STIFFED?

- HOW CAN I RUSH THEM FAST CASH BEFORE LEGAL LIMBO SETS IN?

- HOW DO I DIVIDE EVERYTHING BETWEEN MY SPOUSE AND MY ORIGINAL KIDS?

- WHAT IF THEY ONLY GET ALONG WHEN I'M AROUND?

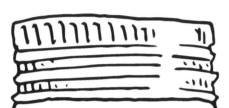

- HOW MUCH SHOULD I LEAVE TO MY STEPKIDS?

- DOES THAT CHANGE HOW MUCH I LEAVE TO MY ORIGINAL KIDS?

- SHOULD I TELL EVERYONE HOW MUCH THEY'RE GOING TO GET?

- OR WILL THEY LOOK AT ME FUNNY FROM THEN ON?

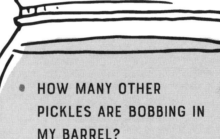

- HOW MANY OTHER PICKLES ARE BOBBING IN MY BARREL?

- WHICH ONES COULD SPEAR US WITH POINTLESS TAXES?

- OR JAR US APART?

- OR SOUR EVERYONE ON ME?

- OR WILL YOU KEEP A-SALTING ME WITH BAD PICKLE-PUNS TILL I SNAP UP EXPERTS WE'LL RELISH?

SPICY PICKLES *FOR THE* UNMARRIED COUPLE

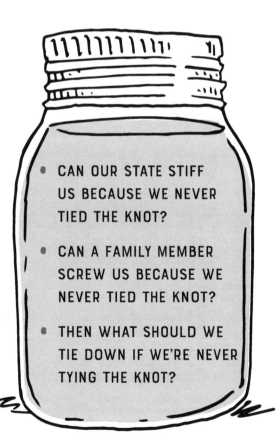

- CAN OUR STATE STIFF US BECAUSE WE NEVER TIED THE KNOT?

- CAN A FAMILY MEMBER SCREW US BECAUSE WE NEVER TIED THE KNOT?

- THEN WHAT SHOULD WE TIE DOWN IF WE'RE NEVER TYING THE KNOT?

- WILL OUR STATE TREAT US AS TOTAL STRANGERS IN THE END?

- WILL I INHERIT NOTHING BUT LOVING MEMORIES?

- WILL I BE KEPT FROM RAISING MY PARTNER'S ORIGINAL KIDS?

- REMIND ME AGAIN WHY WE LIVE IN THIS STATE?

- WOULD EITHER OF US HAVE ENOUGH MONEY TO RAISE OUR KIDS ALONE?
- WOULD EITHER OF US LOSE THE HOUSE?
- WOULD I BE ENTITLED TO **ANYTHING?**
- CAN I CLAIM "COMMON-LAW MARRIAGE" AND HOPE FOR THE BEST?

- HOW MANY OTHER PICKLES ARE BOBBING IN MY BARREL?
- WHICH ONES COULD SPEAR US WITH POINTLESS TAXES?
- OR JAR US APART?
- OR SOUR EVERYONE ON ME?
- OR WILL YOU KEEP A-SALTING ME WITH BAD PICKLE-PUNS TILL I SNAP UP EXPERTS WE'LL RELISH?

SPICY PICKLES

FOR

MULTI-MARRIED

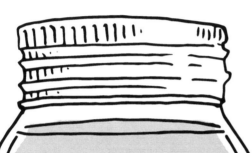

- SHOULD I GENTLY BRING UP A PRENUP OR POST-NUP?

- SHOULD I GENTLY BRING UP KEEPING OUR MONEY SEPARATE?

- SHOULD I GENTLY BRING UP END-OF-LIFE CHOICES?

- SHOULD I GENTLY GRAB MY BLANKET AND TIPTOE TO THE COUCH?

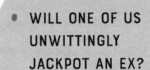

- WILL ONE OF US UNWITTINGLY JACKPOT AN EX?

- IS THE REASON BURIED IN AN OLD DIVORCE DOCUMENT?

- OR A LONG-FORGOTTEN LIFE INSURANCE FOLDER?

- OR A DRAWER FULL OF JUNK MAIL AND KETCHUP PACKETS?

- IS THERE ANY CHANCE MY DEAR SPOUSE COULD LOSE THE HOUSE?

- IS THERE ANY EASIER WAY TO DIVIDE EVERYTHING AMONG EVERYONE?

- IS THERE ANY REASON I SHOULDN'T SIMPLY LET MY FIRSTBORN DECIDE?

- IS THERE ANY CHANCE THIS WILL GO OVER WITH EVERYONE ELSE?

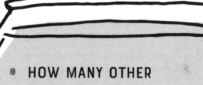

- HOW MANY OTHER PICKLES ARE BOBBING IN MY BARREL?

- WHICH ONES COULD SPEAR US WITH POINTLESS TAXES?

- OR JAR US APART?

- OR SOUR EVERYONE ON ME?

- OR WILL YOU KEEP A-SALTING ME WITH BAD PICKLE-PUNS TILL I SNAP UP EXPERTS WE'LL RELISH?

SPICY PICKLES

FOR THE

KID-FREE

- WHO DO WE LEAVE OUR MONEY TO?
- OUR HOUSE?
- OUR CARS?
- OUR HEIRLOOMS?
- OUR PETS?
- OUR PHOTOS?
- OUR MARBLES?

- WHO'LL BE OUR LEGAL POWERS FOR EVERYTHING?
- WHO'LL CLOSE DOWN OUR HOME FOR US?
- WHO'LL HANDLE OUR FINAL ARRANGEMENTS?
- WHO'LL POINT US TO EXPERTS WHO DO ALL THIS?

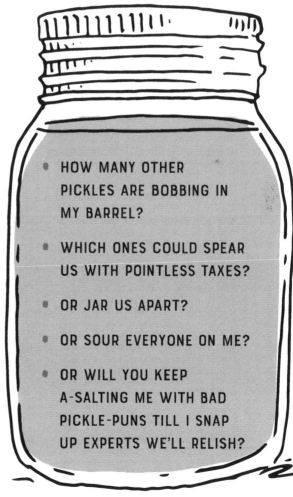

SPICY PICKLES FOR SINGLES

- IF I HAVE PETS, WHAT HAPPENS TO THEM?

- IF I OWN A BUSINESS, WHAT HAPPENS TO THAT?

- IF I PAY CHILD SUPPORT, WHAT HAPPENS THERE?

- IF I HAVE NONE OF THESE, WHY SHOULD I BOTHER?

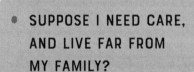

- SUPPOSE I NEED CARE, AND LIVE FAR FROM MY FAMILY?

- SUPPOSE THEY LIVE CLOSE, BUT THEY'RE FAR FROM HELPFUL?

- SUPPOSE I GET INSURANCE TO COVER THIS SITUATION?

- SUPPOSE I COULD ACTUALLY AFFORD IT?

- WHO SHOULD I NAME AS MY LEGAL POWERS?

- WHO SHOULD I NAME AS MY BENEFICIARIES?

- SHOULD I JUST LEAVE EVERYTHING TO MY FAVORITE CHARITIES?

- OR BLOW IT ALL ON A SPACESHIP TO MARS?

- HOW MANY OTHER PICKLES ARE BOBBING IN MY BARREL?

- WHICH ONES COULD SPEAR ME WITH POINTLESS TAXES

- OR SOUR EVERYONE ON ME?

- OR WILL YOU KEEP A-SALTING ME WITH BAD PICKLE-PUNS TILL I SNAP UP EXPERTS I'LL RELISH?

SPICY PICKLES
FOR
LGBTQ+ COUPLES

- WHAT HAPPENS IF THE SUPREME COURT U-TURNS ON SAME-SEX MARRIAGE?

- WILL THE RESPECT FOR MARRIAGE ACT PROTECT US IN OUR STATE?

- OR WON'T IT?

- DO WE HAVE ALL OUR KIDS' CERTIFIED BIRTH CERTIFICATES AND CUSTODY PAPERS?

- DO WE HAVE THE PARENTAGE JUDGMENTS OR ADOPTION DECREES?

- SHOULD WE STOW THEM IN OUR CARRY-ONS WHEN WE TRAVEL?

- DO WE EACH HAVE OUR OWN LIFE INSURANCE, PROPERTY AND BANKING RECORDS AND POWERS OF ATTORNEY?

- WHO GETS MY ORIGINAL KIDS WE'RE RAISING TOGETHER IF SOMETHING HAPPENS TO ME?

- HOW DO WE GUARD AGAINST ANY BLOOD RELATIVES OUT FOR BLOOD?

- HOW MANY OTHER PICKLES ARE BOBBING IN MY BARREL?

- WHICH ONES COULD SPEAR US WITH POINTLESS TAXES?

- OR JAR US APART?

- OR SOUR EVERYONE ON ME?

- OR WILL YOU KEEP A-SALTING ME WITH BAD PICKLE-PUNS TILL I SNAP UP EXPERTS WE'LL RELISH?

SPICY PICKLES
ABOUT
SPECIAL NEEDS

- IS THERE SOME SORT OF TRUST FOR SPECIAL-NEEDS KIDS?

- WOULD SUCH A TRUST BE OUR BEST (OR ONLY) OPTION?

- WILL OUR PLANS KEEP GROWING WITH OUR KIDS?

- WILL OUR BUDGET KEEP GROWING WITH OUR KIDS?

- HOW DO WE KEEP OUR GOVERNMENT BENEFIT LIFELINES GOING?

- HOW MANY FLAMING HOOPS WILL THEY MAKE US JUMP THROUGH?

- HOW HIGH?

- HOW OFTEN?

- IS OUR FIRST CHOICE FOR OUR CHILD'S GUARDIAN THE BEST CHOICE?

- HOW WILL THIS GUARDIAN EVER KNOW OUR CHILD'S SPECIAL ROUTINE?

- COULD FAVORABLE FINANCIAL PLANNING FOR OUR KID TURN OUT LESS THAN FAVORABLE FOR US?

- COULD IT BE LESS THAN FAVORABLE FOR OUR OTHER KIDS, TOO?

- HOW MANY OTHER PICKLES ARE BOBBING IN MY BARREL?

- WHICH ONES COULD SPEAR US WITH POINTLESS TAXES?

- OR JAR US APART?

- OR SOUR EVERYONE ON ME?

- OR WILL YOU KEEP A-SALTING ME WITH BAD PICKLE-PUNS TILL I SNAP UP EXPERTS WE'LL RELISH?

SPICY PICKLES
ABOUT
YOUR KIDS

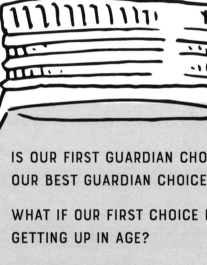

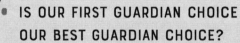

- IS OUR FIRST GUARDIAN CHOICE OUR BEST GUARDIAN CHOICE?

- WHAT IF OUR FIRST CHOICE IS GETTING UP IN AGE?

- OR ACTS RECKLESS WITH MONEY?

- OR IS MARRIED TO A MEATHEAD?

- OR MESSED UP THEIR OWN KIDS?

- OR TURNS US DOWN?

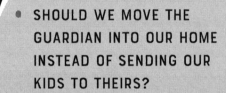

- SHOULD WE MOVE THE GUARDIAN INTO OUR HOME INSTEAD OF SENDING OUR KIDS TO THEIRS?

- SHOULD WE EVER SPLIT UP THE KIDS TO LIVE WITH DIFFERENT GUARDIANS?

- CAN A GUARDIAN OVERRIDE OUR WISHES ON SCHOOLING, RELIGION, NUTRITION, HEALTHCARE?

- HOW DO WE OVERRIDE IT BACK?

- HOW DO WE PLAN FOR OUR KIDS' INHERITANCE ONCE THEY GRADUATE FROM CHILDHOOD?

- HOW DO WE PLAN FOR OUR KIDS' INHERITANCE ONCE THEY GRADUATE FROM US?

- HOW DO WE PLAN FOR OUR KIDS' INHERITANCE ONCE THEY GRADUATE INTO GEEZERS?

- HOW DO WE PROTECT THEIR INHERITANCE AT ANY STAGE FROM HUNGRY CREDITORS?

- HOW MANY OTHER PICKLES ARE BOBBING IN MY BARREL?

- WHICH ONES COULD SPEAR US WITH POINTLESS TAXES?

- OR JAR US APART?

- OR SOUR EVERYONE ON ME?

- OR WILL YOU KEEP A-SALTING ME WITH BAD PICKLE-PUNS TILL I SNAP UP EXPERTS WE'LL RELISH?

SPICY PICKLES

ABOUT

YOUR PETS

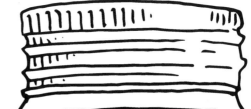

- WHO DO I TRUST TO BE THEIR GUARDIAN?

- WHAT IF NO ONE I KNOW IS RIGHT FOR THEM?

- CAN I NAME MY PET MY HAIRY HEIR?

- CAN I MAKE THEM MY INSURANCE BENEFICIARY?

- WILL THEY END UP IN A SUPER BOWL COMMERCIAL?

- IS THERE SOME SORT OF PET TRUST I CAN SET UP?

- HOW MUCH SHOULD I SET ASIDE TO MAINTAIN THEIR PAMPERED LIFESTYLE?

- SHOULD I LEAVE THIS MONEY TO THEIR GUARDIAN IN ONE LUMP SUM?

- HOW DO I KEEP THAT LUMP FROM TAKING OFF FOR VEGAS?

SPICY PICKLES
for
DEEP POCKETS

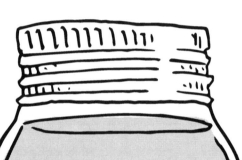

- HOW DO WE DIVIDE UP OUR WEALTH AND NOT DIVIDE UP OUR KIDS?

- HOW DO WE SPLIT UP OUR LUXURY GOODS WITHOUT SPLITTING UP OUR FAMILY?

- HOW DO WE HAND OUT OUR FAMILY HEIRLOOMS WITHOUT GETTING OUR HANDS BITTEN OFF?

- HOW CAN WE KEEP OTHER PEOPLE'S PAWS OFF OUR KIDS' WALLETS?

- SHOULD WE GIFT OUR KIDS TAX-FREE MONEY NOW—OR MAKE THEM WAIT?

- HAVE WE BROUGHT OUR LEGAL, FINANCIAL, INSURANCE AND WEALTH ADVISORS TOGETHER IN ONE ROOM?

- WILL WE HAVE TO FEED THEM?

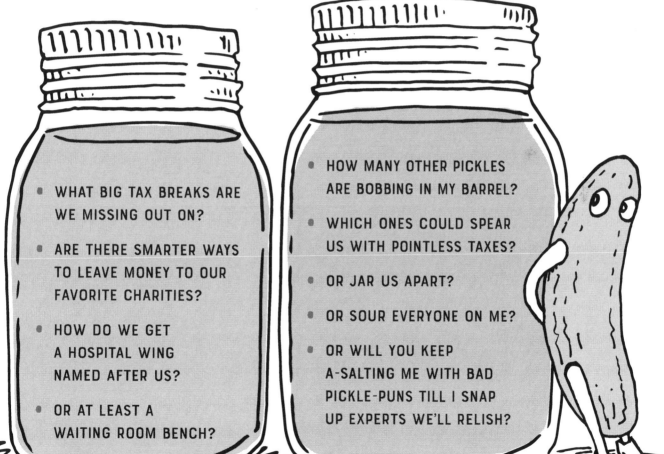

- WHAT BIG TAX BREAKS ARE WE MISSING OUT ON?

- ARE THERE SMARTER WAYS TO LEAVE MONEY TO OUR FAVORITE CHARITIES?

- HOW DO WE GET A HOSPITAL WING NAMED AFTER US?

- OR AT LEAST A WAITING ROOM BENCH?

- HOW MANY OTHER PICKLES ARE BOBBING IN MY BARREL?

- WHICH ONES COULD SPEAR US WITH POINTLESS TAXES?

- OR JAR US APART?

- OR SOUR EVERYONE ON ME?

- OR WILL YOU KEEP A-SALTING ME WITH BAD PICKLE-PUNS TILL I SNAP UP EXPERTS WE'LL RELISH?

SPICY PICKLES
FOR THE
FAMILY BUSINESS

- WHO'LL RUN OUR FAMILY BUSINESS AFTER I'M GONE?

- AND NOT RUN IT INTO THE GROUND?

- IS WHO **RUNS** THE BUSINESS THE SAME AS WHO **OWNS** IT?

- WHAT IF NO ONE WANTS TO DO EITHER?

- IS OUR BUSINESS JUST IN MY NAME?

- DO WE STILL KEEP RECORDS ON SCRAPS OF PAPER?

- DO WE STILL STASH CASH UNDER THE FLOORBOARDS?

- DO WE STILL THINK NOTHING WILL POSSIBLY GO WRONG?

AND MY OWN BIGGEST PICKLE

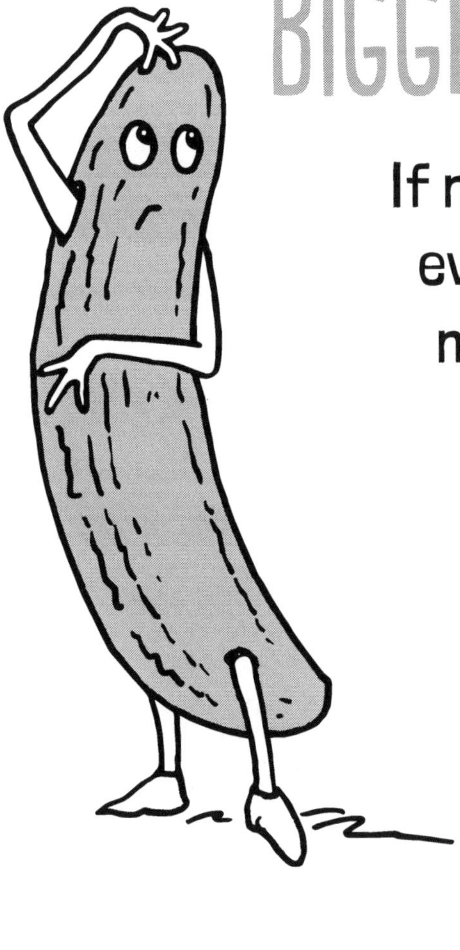

If my able body
ever outlives
my brilliant
mind . . .

. . . what's my brilliant plan?

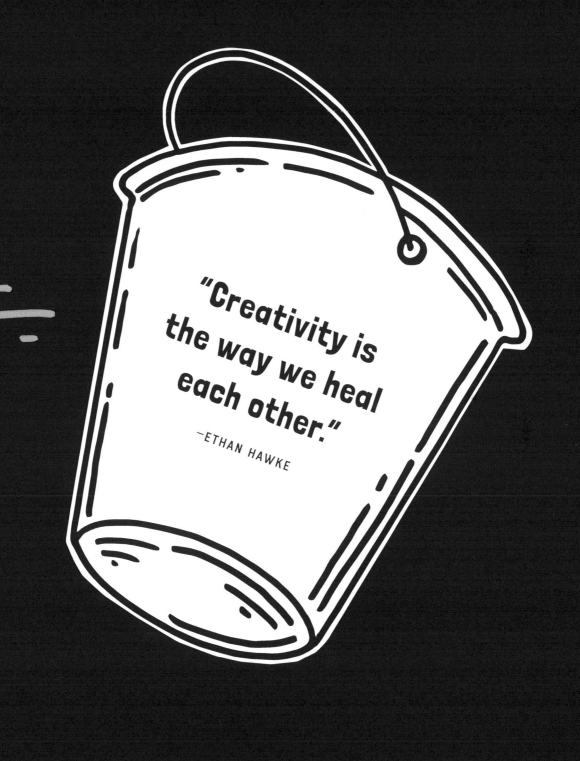

"Creativity is the way we heal each other."

—ETHAN HAWKE

CHAPTER 9

THE FOREVER LETTER

How to love on and on.

- ♥ WARM HUGS FROM DEAR DEPARTED MOM.
- ♥ WORDS OF WISDOM FROM LATE GREAT GRANDDAD.
- ♥ LOVING TEASES FROM A GONE-TOO-SOON SIBLING.

Comfort and connection to hold on to.

The moment you need them.

For the rest of your life.

That's a Forever Letter.

WAIT?! YOU DIDN'T GET ONE?

Then why not respond with your whole heart?

AND WRITE ONE.

IS #FOREVERLETTER TRENDING?

Only since medieval times.

Back then, it was called an "Ethical Will" for parents to hand down moral postulates and ancestral homilies to their yawning kids.

Fortunately, all that puffery's now out, replaced today by anything you're inspired to write to those you love.

To live on with them forever.

DO YOU SAY WHAT THEY'RE INHERITING?

Nope.

That's a job for your Will or Trust.

But this is the ideal place to share your *whys*.

Especially if they're getting much more than expected.

Or much less.

It's really your opening for words left unsaid.

And words you can never say enough.

NOT A WRITER? NO BIG DEAL . . .

Spelling awful? Grammar atrocious? Only your long-gone English teachers would care.

But to your family, your letter will ring true when it sounds like you. *Especially* when it sounds like you.

WHAT DO YOU SAY?

Try spending time with those you'd write to. What do you see? What are their hopes, passions, fears, loves?

Visiting not an option?

Then fly there on a mental field trip, revisiting holidays, occasions, moments together.

Flip through family albums and social media pages, and watch family videos.

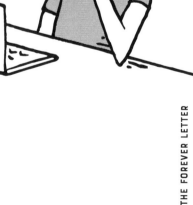

What rises to the top? What *one* most meaningful thought would you want to share?

Start there.

DRAIN ANY VENOM IN YOUR PEN.

Sure, *this one* has it coming.

Yeah, *that one* needs schooling.

No, they can never get back at you.

But they CAN take it out on someone else who doesn't deserve it.

But don't let that stop you.

Go ahead and spill your venom all over the paper.

Then feed it into the shredder.

And leave all paybacks to karma.

SAY NO TO PLAIN WHITE PAPER.

You weren't thinking of using office copy paper, were you?

Not when you can easily get your hands on classy cotton stationery. The kind that's acid-free, so your words won't yellow or fade with time.

Now be a sport, and spring for the matching envelopes, too.

SAY NO TO TIRED TIMES ROMAN.

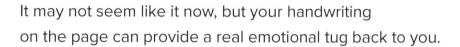

Nothing stands the test of time better than
your own recognizable handwriting.

Even if it's sorta unreadable.

It may not seem like it now, but your handwriting
on the page can provide a real emotional tug back to you.

Just like including photos, poems, doodles, family recipes
and bad jokes you may be famous for.

Or go all out and record a voice-over. Or a video. Or hire
pros to publish a coffee-table hardcover. Or create a
Hollywood-style documentary!

Or . . . just come up with a simple letter.

FINISHED? WHAT NOW?

Sign, seal and tuck your letter away with your Will. You can
always rewrite it someday if you like.

Or, would you rather see their faces as they open it?

Then hand it to them yourself . . . stand aside . . . and watch.

Who knows where true tenderness, frankness and
love can lead?

Forever Letter First-Liners

Take one (or more), please:

My favorite memory of us is _____

My biggest mistake was _____

I lived by a code of _____

I had a wonderful life because _____

The most valuable truth I learned was _____

The toughest challenge I overcame was _____

I feel most grateful for _____

I fulfilled my purpose when _____

What shaped me most was _____

You surely don't know this but _____

Here's what you've meant to me _____

I love you because _____

I wish I'd said this differently _____

I divided the money like that because _____

I'd like you to remember me for _____

You've made me proud because _____

I wish I'd been able to _____

It was secretly me who _____

I will always be with you because _____

All my life, I tried to give you _____

I hope you live out your days by _____

Please try to _____

When I was young, I thought life was _____

I hope you use part of your inheritance to _____

Be sure to reread this letter in times of _____

Don't mourn me (too long) because _____

PHILIP SEYMOUR HOFFMAN

THE CASE OF THE BRAT-WORST.

Everyone knows that trust fund brats can be real wieners. So this Oscar-winning actor came up with an anti-wiener plan that

IGNORED HIS ACCOUNTANT'S ADVICE

thinking it would stop his money from spoiling his kids. After the actor's untimely passing, sure enough, his Will worked as planned. His millions did not spoil his kids.

BUT THEY SURE SPOILED HIS UNCLE.

CHAPTER 10

A CREATIVE FINALE

So many ways to share your love.

Funerals.

We've all squirmed through a few.

On the way home, do you recall thinking something like . . .

YOU CAN GO OUT CLASSIC . . .

Funerals and Memorials are the traditional prayer-and-hymn services we know so well.

Stirring music. Heartfelt eulogies. Warm remembrances.

They're often paired with wakes, shivas or receptions for praying, mourning and sharing, with plenty of comfort food, sympathy dishes and drink to soothe the gathered.

If ritual is your reassurance, go classic.

OR GO OUT CREATIVE . . .

Life Celebrations are fast becoming a new tradition. But what are they?

One big party. (But not THAT kind of party.)

They're uplifting gatherings for sharing stories, music, memories, photos, games—along with tears, joy, laughter, hugging, eating and toasting to the high heavens.

Where no one has to wear their most uncomfortable clothes—or longest face.

If customizing is your comfort, go creative.

CAN YOU MIX CLASSIC WITH CREATIVE?

Sure, if your venue's okay with it.

But if someone in your family isn't, then write out what you want—*and don't want*—while these choices are still yours.

This keeps any unchecked family members from end-running your wishes.

And turning a heartfelt celebration for you into a downer day about them.

WHERE DO YOU WRITE YOUR WISHES?

Where else? On another form.

The Final Arrangements form is free—just search online for one you like.

Then keep it with your Healthcare Directive so it's readily available—and not stowed away with your Will or Trust.

Now it's always on call to keep everybody from guessing what you'd want.

Or doing whatever *they* want.

HOW DO YOU KNOW WHAT YOU'LL WANT?

Doing your own end planning is a once-in-a-lifetime experience.

Unless you know something we don't.

That's where Sendoff Specialists come in—the faith leaders, certified life celebrants, funeral directors and doulas in your area.

More than masters of ceremony, they can help you blend the needs of the day with your creativity, spirituality and dignity to bring your ideas to life someday for your family and friends.

Already have a Sendoff Specialist in mind? Set up a chat.

Need to connect? Seek out someone who's a natural with empathy, compassion, creativity, flexibility.

Who can also make you laugh.

Create *Aha!*

SHOULD YOU PAY NOW—OR LATER?

PAY NOW TO SAVE MONEY. Just don't sign anything till you've read your state's online consumer guide for prepaid arrangements. Could save you a bundle.

PAY LATER TO STAY FLEXIBLE. After all, you can't predict the future. But waiting costs more, and the higher tab will still need to be covered someday. But how?

Your financial planner will see you now.

HOW FAR DO YOU TAKE SENDOFF PREPLANNING?

As far as you're comfortable—but not as far as picking the cocktail napkins.

Rule of Thumb: Many drop a fortune on the forgettable, while others spend far less and get much more.

What's their secret?

Meaning over Money.

So no one goes home thinking, "That was the LAST thing I'd *ever* want."

FINAL TOUCHES

Setting the stage for a
Life Celebration with meaning.

ONCE UPON A TIME . . .

You could only choose between two locations: a house of worship or a funeral home.

Today, you have a third choice:

None of the above.

Which means you can now choose just about any setting you want:

BOWLING ALLEY, BOTANICAL GARDENS, GOLF COURSE, SUNSET CRUISE, PARTY BARGE, FIELD OF DREAMS, MUSEUM, THEATRE, WINERY, PUB, OBSERVATORY, LIBRARY, LOCAL ZOO, HISTORIC MANSION, COUNTRY CLUB, VFW HALL, SCHOOL, BEACH, RESTAURANT, BREWERY, FAVORITE PARK, TAILGATE PARTY, ART GALLERY, FAR-OFF PLACE OF SIGNIFICANCE, OR JUST THE OL' FAMILIAR BACKYARD.

CAN YOU SUM UP YOUR LIFE IN A SONG?

A personal anthem. An uplifting hymn. A lyrical masterpiece.

A tune that's forever to become about you, whisking you to everyone's side the moment it's heard.

For ideas across all musical genres, search 'Top funeral songs of all time.' Or perhaps you'll find your personal best right here:

→ Frank Sinatra's **triumphant** My Way.

→ Eva Cassidy's **stirring** Over the Rainbow.

→ Samuel Barber's **moving** Adagio for Strings.

→ Sinead O'Connor's **Princely** Nothing Compares 2 U.

→ Audrey Assad's **spiritual** Abide with Me.

→ Judy Collins's **amazing** Amazing Grace.

→ Josh Groban's **affecting** You Raise Me Up.

→ Norman Greenbaum's **crowd-pleasing** Spirit in the Sky.

→ Monty Python's **bust-a-gut whistle-along** Always Look on the Bright Side of Life.

→ Or AC/DC's **fiery rabble-rouser** Highway to Hell.

WHAT WILL YOUR OBITUARY SAY ABOUT YOU?

Find out. Write it yourself.

A good obituary is a short story about you with meaning.

It can comfort those closest to you—even uplift those you hardly know.

If you happen to be rich and famous, they'll write yours for you, warts and all.

Everyone else gets to spin it the way they like—then pay for it to appear in a hometown paper and on online memorial sites. Or for free on social media.

Search 'Best self-written obituaries,' and get ready to be inspired by each writer's evergreen words.

Even shed a tear for someone you can never meet.

Perhaps you'll then feel inspired to write your own, taking it out of starchy laundry list and into meaningful narrative of your life.

Or heed investment guru Warren Buffett's sage advice:

"You should write your own obituary—and then try to figure out how to live up to it."

CAN YOU SQUEEZE INTO A ONE-LINER?

A good epitaph should forever bring a smile or tear to those who love you.

And enchant curious passersby, too.

Why let them chisel a tired old saying under your name, when yours can be poetic, inspirational, loving or philosophical.

Or funny, if trending is your eternal wish:

I can finally rest without his snoring. —UNKNOWN WIFE

There goes the neighborhood. —RODNEY DANGERFIELD

You're standing on my boobs. —UNKNOWN

I'm in on a plot. —ALFRED HITCHCOCK

Going! Going!! Gone!!! —AUCTIONEER

I will not be right back after this message. —MERV GRIFFIN

At last—a hole in one. —AMATEUR GOLFER

Here lies my husband—so what else is new? —UNKNOWN

That's all, folks! —MEL BLANC

The next 14 pages contain images and ideas some people may find **too creative.**

Before jumping ahead to page 186, first choose
A or **B** below—tell a trusted family member—
then treat yourself to an ice-cream sundae.

☐ a.   ☐ b.

URN   BOX

"Fill an hourglass with my ashes so I can still join in at family game night."

—UNKNOWN

WHAT'S YOUR DISPOSITION?

Pick one.

IT'S AN ODD SHOPPING LIST, BUT HERE GOES:

CLASSIC EARTH BURIAL. Casket . . . cemetery . . . plot . . . marker . . . daisies.

GREEN BURIAL. Casket without metal and exotic wood. No concrete liner. And no harmful embalming fluid. Or simply a shroud with nothing else.

FLAME CREMATION. Intense heat leads to an urnful of ashes. No casket or embalming fluid. Much more affordable than an earth burial, and now the preferred choice.

SCIENCE DONATION. Body is gifted for research and education to help others live healthier lives. (Not an organ donation, which is different.)

WATER CREMATION. * Peaceful alkaline water bath leads to an urnful of ashes. No casket, embalming fluid, airborne toxins or wasted energy.

NATURAL ORGANIC REDUCTION. * One month of composting with natural materials such as wood chips and alfalfa leads to nutrient-rich soil for a family memorial garden or forest.

DEEP-SEA BURIAL. If it's 3+ nautical miles out and 600+ feet deep, one can sleep with the fishes without seeking permission. Precise geolocation provided for future family visits.

HOME BURIAL. * Choose your own private patch of land to rest in peace—as long as your descendants don't take off for greener pastures.

CRYOGENIC FREEZING. Body is frozen till science can figure out how to thaw it to life. No guarantees. No refunds. No sweaters.

DO NOT DISTURB

*If allowed in your neck of the woods.

THINK OUTSIDE THE (WOODEN) BOX.

MAKE YOUR OWN CASKET. Handy? Build the old standard or create your life's passion, such as these (all real!): electric keyboard, tanning bed, soccer ball, sports car, skateboard, digital camera, wine holder, candy bar— or working roulette table.

DECK OUT A PLAIN CASKET. All thumbs? Personalize any standard casket with stick-ons of your favorite sports teams, guitar heroes, military insignias, selfies— or choose a 360-degree vinyl wrap customized to your personal passions.

SPORT AN ORGANIC MUSHROOM SUIT. This handcrafted mushroom-and-micro-organism robe hastens nature, neutralizes toxins and sends nutrients back to Mother Earth. Made famous by actor Luke Perry in his final role.

ASH LANDINGS

Oh, the places you can go!

GO TRADITIONAL: SCATTERED, RESERVED OR NICHED.

FREEDOM OUTDOORS. Choose a place (or places) of true personal meaning—unless it's Fenway Park, anyplace named Disney, a speeding rollercoaster, or anywhere ill-advised or illegal. Check local laws, so your family won't get your ash handed to them. And leave a note reminding them to stand upwind.

GARDEN SPREADING. Select a landscaped communal garden in a dedicated section of some cemeteries. Perfect for peaceful family visits and quiet meditation.

URN AT HOME. Whether you're destined for living room mantel, hallway curio cabinet, or shelf in a closet, browse the array of artistic, inventive and kitschy urns online for one that speaks to you. Protip: leave a someday scattering plan.

THINK VERTICAL. Reserve a private wall niche—a sort of 'high-rise condo' columbarium—located in many cemeteries and houses of worship.

GO CREATIVE: NEW, WILD OR BIZARRE.

GET YOUR RHYTHM ON. Ashes are pressed into a vinyl record, then grooved with your favorite tunes—or your cringeworthy karaoke.

 SHINE ON, YOU CRAZY DIAMOND. A bit of ash is pressed into a stunning, wearable diamond—in the cut, color and carat weight you spring for.

HANG AROUND THE HOUSE. Ashes are blended into paint pigments so an artist can put more of you into your own smiling portrait.

SPROUT AS TREE-MAINS. Ashes are mixed with tree seeds in a biodegradable planter, so you can grow into a huggable tree.

BOND WITH BLING. A dash of ash is set into a handcrafted locket, to keep you close to your loved one's heart.

BUILD-IT-YOURSELF URN. Be embraced by your life's true love, like some folks who crafted for themselves an oversized golf ball, martini glass, whiskey bottle, sewing machine, working hourglass—even a scale model of the USS *Enterprise*.

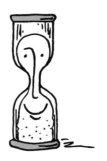

CREATE A STEALTH URN. Hollow out a plush huggable teddy bear or suitable work of art—so only those close to you will know you're nearby. Or add ashes to large colorful maracas, and hand them out for a family memorial jam session.

GET UNDER SOMEONE'S SKIN. A tattoo artist blends special inks with your treated ash, so you can forever touch someone who must really love you.

FRAME YOUR BODY ART. Arrange to have your loudest, proudest tattoo preserved, framed and presented to your family. You read that right.

MUSIC TO THEIR EARS. Crystal windchimes are bonded with ash, so every breeze can chime out a comforting (or haunting) hello.

ART TO THEIR EYES. Ash is fused into a colorful glass heart, orb or starfish, and set atop a gently glowing base to light the way in the dark.

BE TEED OFF. A touch of ash is preserved atop a sleek glass-domed golf tee. But don't take this to the fairway— they're nearly a hundred bucks each!

GO NATURAL: EARTH, WIND, FIRE OR WATER.

SELECT A FAMILY TREE. Own a majestic tree in a protected memorial forest for the ashes of your family together with your pets. A peaceful place in nature for family visits.

TAKE A DIVE. Ashes are bonded to an eco-friendly reef ball, then lowered onto the seabed for healthier coral and fish. Family visits by snorkel or scuba.

HONOR AT SEA. The U.S. Navy and Coast Guard provide no-cost sea scatterings for military personnel, retirees, veterans and their dependents. Families stay ashore, though.

SWIM WITH THE FISHES. Ashes are spread onto the water from a special charter boat during a private onboard memorial.

BE ONE WITH THE SEA. A float-off-gracefully-and-sink-on-its-own biodegradable urn takes the place of ashes bobbing around on the water's surface.

BE ONE WITH THE SKY. A biodegradable balloon silently lifts ashes into the air, bursting at six miles high and freeing them to the four winds.

GET STONED. Ashes are transformed into polished, palm-sized art stones for displaying, caressing or skimming.

GET BLASTED. Confetti and streamers are mixed with ashes to be shot by special cannon 70 feet skyward for a colorful daytime fireworks display.

FLAP ON THE WING. Ashes are placed inside a custom birdhouse for local birds to scatter when they fly off for nesting and nourishment.

Create *Aha!* Last Bucket List .com

RECEIVE A 21-GUN SALUTE. Live shot shells or cartridges are hand-filled with ashes for skeet shooting, hunting—or a patriotic sendoff.

BE AN EASY RIDER. Vroom off into sunsets together forever with this handcrafted, triple-chrome-plated urn that's bolted to your partner's hog.

BURST FORTH. Go out in the rocket's red glare during a dazzling display of fireworks that light up the night sky.

GO GLOBAL. Ask your loved ones to scatter a share of your ashes in places of meaning to you around the world—or stay nearby in your own cemetery plot.

HIRE A PROFESSIONAL MOURNER. Who IS that mysterious weeper dressed entirely in black and standing all alone?? It's your little secret to take to the grave.

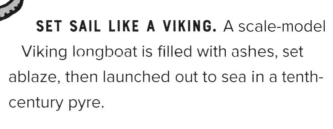

SET SAIL LIKE A VIKING. A scale-model Viking longboat is filled with ashes, set ablaze, then launched out to sea in a tenth-century pyre.

SCATTER FROM 10,000 FEET. Ask a gutsy loved one to jump out of a plane for a high-altitude scattering in tandem with a licensed skydiving pro.

FLYOVER SALUTE. Earthbound loved ones witness a trail of ashes pour out the back of a specially outfitted plane. Thrill points: Choose the Spitfire.

ROCKET TO THE GREAT BEYOND. Launch your ashes into orbit on a two-year mission that re-enters like a shooting star—or break free of earth's bounds on an eternal deep-space voyage, like *Star Trek*'s James "Scotty" Doohan, Nichelle "Lt. Uhura" Nichols, and series creator Gene Roddenberry, along with several fans of the show.

Create *Aha!*

PROTIPS

The Finale

★ An uplifting Life Celebration with meaning begins the healing.

★ Laughter—once thought inappropriate—can be just as healing as tears.

★ Simple plans will ease the lives of those carrying out your wishes.

★ So will money. Fund what needs funding.

✷ Veteran honors? Only if you can locate proof of honorable active military service.

✷ Put all your choices into a Final Arrangements form, and say what's already paid for.

✷ Your form stays together with your Healthcare Directive — not with your Will or Trust.

✷ A Final Arrangements form is free — just search online for one you like.

"Every secret
has an
expiration date."

—JOSIYAH MARTIN

WHO KNEW?

Ways to keep your secretest secrets secret.

LOVE LETTERS IN A DUSTY SHOEBOX

JUICY JPEGS IN A **PHONY FOLDER.**

FRISKY SILICONE IN A NIGHTSTAND DRAWER.

Everyone keeps secrets.

But what will become of yours after you're gone?

They'll go from well-guarded stash to unguarded trash.

Becoming easy pickins for housekeepers, inspectors, movers, cops, robbers . . .

And the family snoops you hid them from in the first place.

THE 3 FATES OF UNGUARDED SECRETS.

Once your hidden stash loses its sole defender, all you can do is hope that it:

1. Falls into the trash and heads straight to the landfill.

2. Falls into the donation box and doesn't show up on eBay.

3. Falls into the hands of the right relative who keeps their big mouth shut.

But what if it's the wrong relative?

You could easily become the Thanksgiving turkey your family carves up that year.

And every year after that.

DON'T WANT TO BE THE TURKEY?

Then deputize a Cleaner.

Not the *Pulp Fiction* type, but a trusted crony with cat-like cool who'll sneak in to gather up your intimate letters, questionable pastimes, and any other secrets—and make them all disappear. Then seal their lips forever.

CLUE IN YOUR TRUSTED CLEANER.

Unless this person lives with you, there'll be no waltzing in once you're not there to open the door.

So prepare to hand over any keys, passwords, alarm codes, combinations and security clearances they'll need.

Dog treats, too. Just in case.

And a treasure map to your stash.

But what'll they uncover once they get there?

Only intimate or embarrassing? Or ill-gotten and illegal?

The sort of things that can turn a faithful accomplice into an unwitting accessory.

Which leads to another question . . .

What kind of life are you leading anyway?

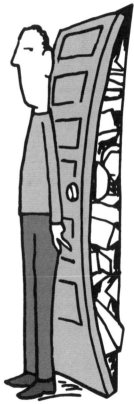

OH, AND ONE LAST OPTION.

Just take care of this yourself.

While you still can.

FLORENCE
GRIFFITH
JOYNER

THE CASE OF THE HOTFOOTING HEIRS.

After becoming wealthy and famous, the fastest female Olympian of all time called her lawyer and set up her Will. She then

SECURELY TUCKED IT AWAY

to be sure it stayed safe. But when Flo-Jo died at the young age of 38, no one could find her Will. No matter where they looked, they came up empty. Which left them only one option: Break Flo-Jo's record

RACING TO THE COURTHOUSE.

CHAPTER 12

THE DIGITAL AFTERLIFE

From in the cloud
. . . to high above.

EVER BEEN PUNKED BY A POP-IN
STARRING A LOVED ONE YOU LOST?

NOW . . .
WHAT WAS THE QUESTION AGAIN?

HOW TO POP CLUELESS POP-INS.

Just ask the person in the pop-in to change their social media settings—provided they're not off resting in peace.

Because then it falls to their family to change their settings, secure their financial assets, rescue digital valuables, and set the fate of each account.

Which might even be against the law for them to do.

When platforms don't want antsy heirs nosing around in other people's business.

WHO OWNS YOUR STUFF IN THE CLOUD?

You do . . . *right?*

Nice try.

Go again.

Who owns all the pictures, videos, writings, music, art, spreadsheets, emails, URLs, backups and personal embarrassments you send to that puffy white vapor in the sky?

You do . . . *maybe?*

WAIT . . . THEY MIGHT OWN WHAT'S YOURS??

Do you remember clicking "AGREE" when you signed up for each platform?

Do you remember reading the legal Terms of Service you'd just agreed to?

NO? Luckily, you've still got an ace up your sleeve.

You're alive to fix it.

DEFEND YOUR AFTERLIFE . . . WHILE YOU CAN.

Create a "Digital Will"—an open kimono on your entire digital life.

Here you write in all your password-protected places, saying what you want done with each of them someday.

You then deputize a "Digital Watchdog" to see this through—someone good with computers, passwords and trust. Especially trust.

Now you'll keep your loose ends from dangling.

Kindly close that kimono now.

3 STEPS TO CREATING YOUR DIGITAL WILL.

1. GATHER YOUR PASSWORDS.

Have you already saved them in a password manager app? Good! Proceed to Step 2.

Are they all saved on scraps of paper scattered around the house? *Um* . . . there goes your weekend.

2. DECODE THEIR RULES.

Start by googling this doozy: *"What happens to my Facebook account if I die?"*

Up comes everything you never wanted to know about Facebook policy on Legacy Contacts, digital treasure downloading, account memorializing, and all that jazz.

Now repeat this for every important password-protected site where you spend (or squander) your time.

3. SET YOUR INSTRUCTIONS.

Fill in your Digital Will, including what you want preserved, downloaded or deleted.

(Like a freaky browser history, perhaps?)

Now hand your sealed Digital Will to your Digital Watchdog on the way to a nice dinner. On you.

MEET YOUR DIGITAL AFTERLIFE GREETERS.

Hold on. . . . What's that they're sniffing?

Your most valuable accounts.

And if they catch a whiff of no-one-there, they'll unleash their spidery software to swipe your identity, steal your money, and blast the smarmiest, scammiest spam to everyone you ever knew.

From you.

Your Digital Will can protect your family and your treasures from these hackers.

Because your Digital Watchdog can make it look like somebody's home. Or seal it off. Or shut it down.

And send these digital no-goodniks packing, with a fitting and proper goodbye from you:

SNIFF OFF!

PROTIPS

Digital Afterlife

- Here we say "Digital Watchdog" instead of the stodgy "Digital Executor."

- Passwords in your Digital Will stay secret, while passwords in your Trust or Will do not.

- Keep the Digital Will original with your Trust or Will. Give copies to your Digital Executor, lawyer and you.

Not writing in the Master Password of your password manager app is a blunder you'll long be remembered for.

Same goes for any missing passwords to get into your phone, computer and tablet.

Update your Digital Will whenever you update your passwords.

Clouds tend to blow away. Create hard-drive backups of your digital valuables at home.

"The problem with the future is that it keeps turning into the present."

—BILL WATTERSON

CHAPTER 13

YOUR BIG REWARD

Waiting for you at the finish line.

WOWZA!!

What's the big reward??

"Peace of mind," replies the lawyer.

"Peace of mind," repeats the banker.

"Peace of mind," re-repeats the financial planner.

Pfffft.

Where's the joy? Adventure? Pleasure? Fun?

Don't you deserve that, too??

YES YOU DO!

So go dream it up.

And drop it off at the finish line.

AND YOU'RE OFF . . .

Who's readier than you?

BRAVO.

YOU ACED STEP ONE.

YOU'RE CLEARED FOR STEP TWO.

PUMPED WITH CREATIVITY.

PREPPED WITH INSIGHT.

PRIMED TO INSPIRE.

SO WILL-UP YOUR WILLPOWER.

BEFORE YOU TALK YOURSELF OUTTA THIS.

Step Two starts here:

1. FILL OUT A HEALTHCARE DIRECTIVE [40]

2. REGISTER AT DONATE LIFE [58]

3. CHAT WITH A GOOD FINANCIAL PLANNER.

4. DREAM UP MISSIONS OF MEANING [102]

5. CHOOSE AN ESTATE-PLANNING LAWYER [17]

6. THINK UP YOUR FOREVER LETTER(S) [148]

7. TALK TO A SENDOFF SPECIALIST [164]

8. START YOUR DIGITAL WILL [198]

9. TIE YOUR SIGNED PAPERS IN A BOW.

10. REWARD YOURSELF BIG-TIME.

HUH??

What did your lawyer just say?

Decedent
[di·SEE·dent]
One who's no longer alive.

Disinherit
[DIS·in·HAIR·it]
To remove unwanted heirs.

Intestate
[in·TESS·tayt]
Passing without a Will.

Escheat
[es·CHEAT]
State gets all your property.

Property
[PRAH·pur·tee]
Not just real estate—all you own.

Heir
[AIR]
Someone entitled to your property.

Spendthrift
[SPEND·thrift]
The family squanderer.

Fiduciary
[feh·DOUCHY·airy]
Advisor who puts your
interests first.

Per capita / Per stirpes
[purr KAPPA·tuh / purr STUR·peez]
You and fate deciding how to
divvy up inheritances.
(Your lawyer will explain.)

Residuary
[ri·ZIDGE·oo·werry]
Leftovers at the end
of your Will.

Precatory
[PREK·uh·tory]
A hope-to—not a must-do.

Codicil
[KAH·duh·sill]
A legal "P.S." you add later
to your Will.

Dikigorosophobia
[DIE·key·gor·osso·FO·be·yuh]
Fear of lawyers.

ABOUT THE AUTHOR

RICH LIPPMAN is a why-to thinker in a how-to world. In addition to ghostwriting bestsellers, he's published a variety of humorous why-to's on fearless flying for kids, impressive date-night cooking for singles, and even how to sweet-talk your way out of a speeding ticket. Rich grew up near Shea Stadium, and now lives near Dodger Stadium. He's not Mr. Lippman from *Seinfeld*.

ABOUT THE ILLUSTRATOR

DENNIS GORIS has spent too many years slaying dragons in the creative world. As a graphic designer, business owner and cartoonist, he believes most problems can be solved with a heaping teaspoon of silliness. He grew up in Buffalo, NY, and now lives outside Washington, D.C. Say hi at *instagram.com/dennisgoris/.*

THANK YOU

Experts, beta readers, know-it-alls
& unindicted co-conspirators.

SENIOR EDITOR
Joe Azar · *newtwist.press*

LEGAL CONSULTANT
Clayton Cruse · *theestateesq.com*

DESIGNER
Kate Basart · *unionpageworks.com*

EXPERTS
Raymond W. Huang, MD · Internal medicine, geriatrics, palliative & continuing care services
Paul Malley · President, Aging with Dignity *agingwithdignity.org*
Hilary Kleine · VP Communications & Registry, Donate Life America *donatelife.net*
Dan Morilak · Financial Advisor
Steve Neuder · Hospice Chaplain & Pastor
David S.Rosenblatt · SSG Web Services *ssgwebservices.com*
Linda Stuart · Life-Cycle Celebrant *linda-stuart.ca*
Joe Kissell · Publisher, Take Control Books *takecontrolbooks.com*
Deb Leopold · Social Media Manager *@MagicDebsWeb*
Dave · The Corporate Compliance Complier
Jennifer Werthman · Education Director · Cremation Association of North America
  cremationassociation.org
Michael Jauchen · Proofreader · *michael-jauchen.com*
Alex Castro, RN · Owner/CFO Calstro Hospice, Inc. · *calstrohospiceinc.com*

BETA READERS & ADVISORS
Lisa Lippman
Donna Johnston
Andy Lippman
Bill Cates
Lisa Gates
Julia Newhouse
Dennis Jay
Catherine Springer
John Atikian
Rebecca Kimber

Dusty Proctor
Melissa Moulton-Church
Pam McCormick
Lorraine Beltran
Chip Heller
Cindy Warden
Sheri Galan
Elizabeth Hansen
Rick Harrison
Rosa Cheeseman

Stephen Ross
Julie Funk
Eddie Shleyner
Martin Wilsey
Helen O'Brien
Linda Morales
Hayley O'Brien
Stacy Lopez
Mike O'Brien
Sadie Allison

INSPIRATION
Ro & Shel, Stewart A. Williams, Tom Petty, Seth Godin

INTERPLAY

 Last Bucket List   @LastBucketList YourLastBucketList

Create "Aha!"

If you were inspired by this book,
please review it on Amazon for others in need
of a creative jumpstart. Thank you!

Raves about Last Bucket List

I love-love-love this book. It easily digests this complex and often boring topic— and it's hilarious!

Dana A. Blue
Estate Planning Attorney

Powerful stuff. A way to show love and compassion—and this is definitely one way to do that.

Benjamin Diaz
Your Lot & Parcel

A lighthearted read for estate advisors to consider gifting to clients who are procrastinating on end-of-life plans.

Financial Planning Magazine

A good fun guide. Opens the mind to being creative about how you want to be remembered.

David Edey
Executor Help

Create Double "Aha!"

Give a copy of **Last Bucket List**
to someone who needs it—and doesn't know it!

Visit LastBucketList.com

Live long and prosper.

26551273R00126